TRUE
SPORT
STORIES

TRUE SPORT STORIES

Tim Lardner

Illustrated by David Wyatt

Hippo

Scholastic Children's Books,
Scholastic Publications Ltd,
7–9 Pratt Street, London NW1 0AE, UK

Scholastic Inc.,
555 Broadway, New York, NY 10012-3999, USA

Scholastic Canada Ltd,
123 Newkirk Road, Richmond Hill,
Ontario, Canada L4C 3G5

Ashton Scholastic Pty Ltd,
P O Box 579, Gosford, New South Wales,
Australia

Ashton Scholastic Ltd,
Private Bag 94407, Greenmount, Auckland,
New Zealand

First published by Scholastic Publications Ltd, 1995
Copyright © Tim Lardner, 1995
Illustrations copyright © David Wyatt, 1995

ISBN 0 590 55792 0

Typeset by TW Typesetting, Midsomer Norton, Avon
Printed by Cox & Wyman Ltd, Reading, Berks.

10 9 8 7 6 5 4 3

Contents

INTRODUCTION

Sport provokes every kind of human emotion. One moment you're up, the next you're down; one match you're a winner, the next you're a loser. Whether it is Wimbledon or Wembley, a local gymkhana or the Olympic Games, sport can make you ecstatically happy, helpless with laughter, or bring you to the depths of despair.

Some of these stories show how people from difficult backgrounds have excelled in their chosen sport, often overcoming major setbacks on their journey to fame. This is true of swimmer Dawn Fraser and sprinter Wilma Rudolph, and true, too, of boxer Muhammad Ali and tennis-player Pancho Gonzales. Other personalities, like skier Eddie Edwards and marathon runner Felix Carvajal, are more unlikely heroes, but their stories are fascinating nevertheless.

The stories also show sport's unpredictability. Who could have guessed the events that lay in store when a dog strayed on to a football pitch or spectators turned up to see a game on a foggy day? Each time a starting pistol fires, or a referee's whistle blows, there's no knowing what's about to happen.

Sport offers us so much to watch, enjoy and talk about. These true stories are examples of sport's incredible capacity to amaze, delight or dismay.

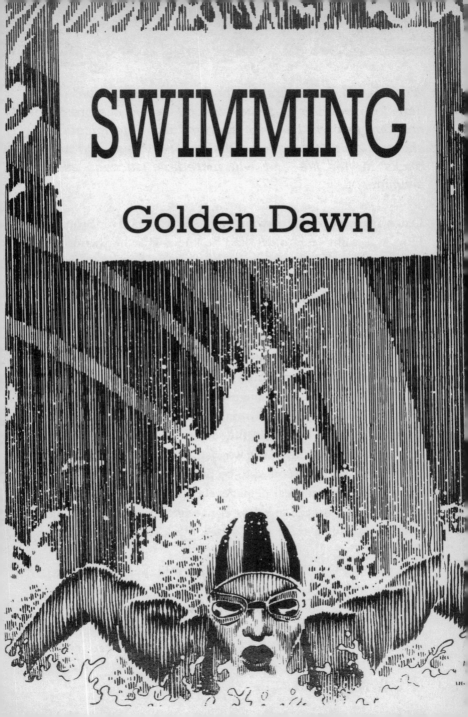

SWIMMING

Golden Dawn

When Dawn Fraser first learned to swim, she could not have foreseen the tragedies which fate had in store for her. But, through her own courage and determination, she was able to overcome the great sorrows and setbacks in her life and win incredible success as a swimmer...

Dawn Fraser learned to swim when she was six. Her brother, Don, was eight years older, and he knew what he was doing when he let go and left her in deep water in the swimming pool. He watched her closely as she fought through the water to the edge of the pool with panicky strokes.

Dawn was angry with Don that day. She thought he should have carried her through the water on his back. But she was soon grateful to him. She was on her way to becoming a unique swimming champion.

Dawn Fraser was the youngest of a family of eight children living in Balmain, an industrial suburb of Sydney, one of Australia's largest cities. On the face of it, Dawn didn't seem cut out to be a swimmer: she was asthmatic and had an allergy to chlorine. But she refused to be put off. In fact, Dawn soon found swimming a great help. As she improved her breathing in the water, she became less concerned about her asthma. She spent all her spare time at the outdoor Elkington Park Baths.

As a child, Dawn was tall, slim and wild. She was a determined girl, but she faced her first tragedy when she was 13 years old. Her brother Don became terminally ill with leukaemia. She was very close to Don. He had encouraged her enthusiasm for sport, and he and Dawn had a lot in common.

When Don died, he was only 21 years old.

"Keep on with the swimming, kid," he had told Dawn shortly before he died. "You never know, you could finish up a champ."

On the day of Don's death, Dawn cycled to the local pool, found a sheltered spot and sat down and wept. She felt very alone. Soon afterwards she decided to give everything she had to swimming.

When she was 15 Dawn joined a coach called Harry Gallagher in Adelaide. It was a long way from home. She missed her family, she missed Sydney, but swimming made up for what she missed. She worked as a shopgirl but she ate, drank and slept swimming. She worked hard on the rhythm of her swimming stroke and got faster and faster.

In 1955 Dawn Fraser competed in the Australian National Championships. She didn't do very well in the 110 yards freestyle, but was determined to do better in the 220 yards freestyle. She set off fast and streaked ahead of the other swimmers. "She'll blow up soon," somebody said. But she didn't. She won the event by seven metres in two minutes 29.5 seconds, a new Australian record.

The next year she did even better in the National Championships. Her main rival was Lorraine Crapp, who was younger than Dawn but had already broken five world records. Lorraine beat Dawn in the 440 yards freestyle, but it was a different story over the shorter distances. In front of 3,000 people, Dawn won the 110 yards freestyle by half a metre, with breathtaking speed. The world record of 64.6 seconds had stood for twenty years. Now it was 64.5 seconds and held by Dawn Fraser.

Melbourne, Australia, December 1956

Her rise to the top was just in time for the 1956 Olympics in Melbourne. They began in December, during the Australian summer, but Dawn Fraser nearly missed them! She went into hospital suffering from earache, an eye infection and bad headaches. This was only a few days before the Olympics. Fortunately she recovered quickly and swam her way to the final of the 100 metres freestyle.

She was expected to win, but the night before the final was unforgettable. Dawn had a nightmare: "The gun went off but I had honey on my feet and it was hard to pull them away from the starting-block. I finally fought free and dived high … It seemed a long time before I hit the water, and the water wasn't water; it was spaghetti. I fought with it, and kept going up and down in the one place, like a yo-yo. The spaghetti strands tangled and tied my feet, and I was swimming with my arms alone. Of course I fouled up the turn and took a few mouthfuls, and I woke up gasping and fighting in a sea of spaghetti."

The final took place late in the evening. It meant a long, long day of waiting. Dawn had plenty of time to get nervous. She walked around the pool and got to know it. She rehearsed the race in her own mind. She imagined the waves in the pool as the swimmers ploughed through the water. She knew it would be worse in the centre lanes, where she would be swimming. On the bus to the pool that night, Dawn was shaking. She was nervous but excited, confident but afraid. She felt awful.

"I feel as though I'm waiting for an execution – my own execution," she told her coach as she waited for the start.

Some of the other swimmers dropped into the pool to flex their muscles. Dawn stayed on dry land, limbering up as best she could.

The eight finalists mounted their blocks. The starter watched and waited. Silence. Then the sound of the gun. The swimmers tensed their muscles and plunged forward, and the glassy stillness of the water was shattered. All Dawn's nerves disappeared as she hit the water and settled into her relaxed, rhythmic swimming stroke, but Lorraine Crapp had got away first.

A 100-metres race means two lengths of the pool. On the outward journey Dawn caught Lorraine Crapp, but Lorraine turned faster and pushed away with a lead of a metre. Dawn swam hard. The two Australian girls were stroke for stroke, side by side. They stayed stroke for stroke right to the end, touching the edge virtually together. Neither knew who had won. They turned round and watched the race for third place. They saw Faith Leech get the touch for third. She was Australian too.

Lorraine and Dawn lay on their backs, hung on to the cork ropes and floated. Then an official came and stood by Dawn. He winked and held up one finger. She had won. Dawn and Lorraine hugged each other. They couldn't speak.

"It looks like a world record," somebody said. The time was 62.0 seconds.

"It makes our relay team look pretty good," said Lorraine.

Lorraine was right. The relay team won the gold, so Dawn ended her first Olympics with two gold medals.

That first gold medal would always be very special. Dawn stood on the victory rostrum and tears rolled down her cheeks, her hand clutching the gold medal that hung round her neck. She borrowed a ladder from a television crew and climbed up to the stand to see her mother and father in the audience.

"It was Don's race, Mum," said Dawn, thinking of the brother who taught her to swim. "I won it for him."

Dawn went on to win the 440 yards and 110 yards freestyle races at the 1958 Empire and Commonwealth Games. More and more records and victories came her way.

However, in 1959 Dawn became ill with hepatitis, which meant a whole year away from serious swimming and competing. True to form, Dawn fought her way back to fitness.

Then came more world records and more gold medals.

At the 1960 Australian Championships she broke an incredible three world records inside 45 minutes, including the 100 yards butterfly, an event Dawn was completely new to. The announcer could hardly conceal his delight: "You have just seen the greatest performance by any woman athlete, in any sport, the world has ever known." Later in the National Championships, Dawn Fraser knocked three seconds off another world record – the 220 yards freestyle.

Rome, Italy, August 1960

In Rome, at the 1960 Olympics, Dawn made history by becoming the first woman to defend an Olympic swimming title. After her swim, clutching a teddy-bear mascot and her third gold medal, she again cried tears of joy at her success.

The following year brought more tears but this time they were tears of sadness. Dawn's father died after a long illness.

Dawn had been working hard on her 100 metres freestyle speed. She wore tighter and lighter swimsuits. She shaved her legs and arms. She had her hair cut short. But most importantly, she continually worked on the smoothness of her freestyle stroke, gliding through the water. The magic 60-second barrier was within her grasp. Eventually, in the trials for the 1962 Empire and Commonwealth Games, she clocked 59.9 seconds. She went on to win four gold medals at those Games in Perth: 110 yards freestyle, 100 yards freestyle relay, the medley relay and the 440 yards freestyle.

Then came 1964: a year of tragedy; a year of glory.

Dawn started the year in great form. At the National Championships in February she won the 110 yards freestyle in 58.9 seconds and the 220 yards in exactly two minutes.

She stayed in Sydney after the Championships and enjoyed some time with her family. One night Dawn went to a rugby club dinner. She drove home at about eleven o'clock in a borrowed car. Her mother and sister were in the back seat, a friend in the front. She drove round a curve in the road at about forty miles per hour to find a parked lorry in their path.

"Look out, Dawn!" screamed her friend beside her. But it was too late.

She braked, swerved and felt the impact of the sickening crash.

Dawn regained consciousness lying on the grass verge to discover that her mother and sister had been taken to hospital. Her friend was bleeding from cuts on her face. Dawn passed out again shortly afterwards.

When Dawn came round again, in hospital, she found out that she had a chipped vertebra and would be laid up for months. Then came tragic news. Her mother had died in the crash. Dawn was devastated. Words cannot describe how despondent she felt in the days and weeks that followed. She had lost her mother now, as well as her father and brother, and her swimming career seemed to be finished.

Her neck was in a steel brace for nine weeks while the bone began to heal. One day in autumn 1964 she put on a swimsuit and, still wearing her neck brace, walked to the swimming pool. She thought she would have a chat to some of her friends at the pool, but when she got there she couldn't resist the water. She took off the brace and slid gently into the pool. She couldn't swim freestyle because she couldn't turn her head. Instead she swam breaststroke ... and it felt wonderful.

Swimming had always helped Dawn to relax and she wanted to do it again. With the help of neck massages and muscle exercises, she went back into training. She set her heart on breaking 61 seconds and getting into the Australian Olympic team. She did it. She was on her way to Japan for her third Olympics.

Tokyo, Japan, October 1964

By now the world scene had changed. The rising star was Sharon Strouder of the USA. But Dawn recovered enough to make the final. Surely it was asking too much of her to win for the third time ... or was it?

Dawn went ahead in the first length of the final, but turned slowly because she wouldn't use a tumble-turn. She lost the lead. At 70 metres, Strouder was still with her. But Dawn was a great competitor. She wasn't someone who enjoyed racing against the clock on her own. It was competition that spurred her on to faster times. Dawn slowly pulled away … and won by a metre. It was her third successive 100 metres Olympic title and her fourth gold medal. This last one was for her mother and father.

• In three Olympics, Dawn Fraser won a total of four gold medals and four silver medals.

• Dawn was the first person to defend an Olympic title twice, although discus thrower Al Oerter equalled her feat only two days after Dawn had won her gold medal at the 1964 Olympics. Oerter won the discus gold in 1956, 1960, 1964 and 1968. Like Fraser, he survived a bad car accident (in 1957). He won his third gold medal while seriously injured.

• During her career, Dawn Fraser broke 27 world records and was the first woman to swim 100 metres in under a minute. She was awarded the MBE in 1967 in recognition of her achievements.

• Dawn moved on to politics in later life. Between 1988 and 1991 she served as an elected member of the New South Wales state parliament.

Swimming

1. Australian Shane Gould won an incredible five swimming medals at the 1972 Munich Olympics: three golds, a silver and a bronze.

2. American Mark Spitz beat even Shane Gould's record, winning seven gold medals in swimming events at the 1972 Munich Olympics.

3. In 1976, Kornelia Ender equalled Dawn Fraser's women's swimming record of four Olympic gold medals. Fraser's amazing record of eight Olympic women's swimming medals was equalled by two others – Kornelia Ender and Shirley Babashoff.

4. At the 1960 Olympic Games, Australian John Devitt won a gold medal in the 100 metres freestyle. This must have come as a surprise, since he actually came *second*, to Lance Larson of America. Despite the evidence of photo-finish cameras, electronic timers and officials, the chief judge awarded the gold to John Devitt – a controversial decision to say the least, and one which has never been explained.

5. British swimmer Adrian Moorhouse had won Olympic gold and several European and Commonwealth titles in the breaststroke, and had three world records to his credit. At the world

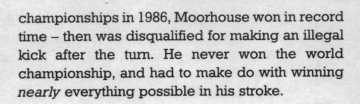

championships in 1986, Moorhouse won in record time – then was disqualified for making an illegal kick after the turn. He never won the world championship, and had to make do with winning *nearly* everything possible in his stroke.

6. Besides swimming pool competitions, there is a history of marathon swimmers tackling dangerous waters and pioneering routes. The first man to swim the English Channel was Captain

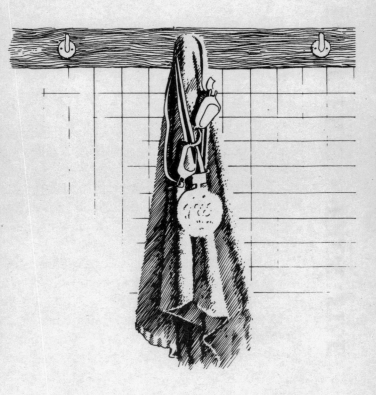

Matthew Webb in August 1875. He later drowned while trying to swim across the rapids above Niagara Falls. In August 1981, Jon Erikson, a 26-year-old American, swam the English Channel three times without stopping.

LONG DISTANCE RUNNING
The Dusty Marathon

In the days before sponsorship and television coverage anyone could just turn up and take part in the Olympic Games. A Cuban postman's amazing stamina and dedication led him to do just that, and in the toughest Olympic event – the marathon...

St Louis, Missouri, USA, 30 August 1904

Felix Carvajal was one of the most unusual people ever to run an Olympic marathon. A postman on the island of Cuba, he began to enjoy running while he was delivering letters. He heard about the Olympic Games and thought he stood a chance of winning the marathon. All Felix needed was the money to get to St Louis, USA, where the Games were being held.

He raised money for his journey by staging exhibitions in Cuba. To attract attention to his running skills, he ran round the public square in Havana until a crowd gathered. Then he mounted a soap-box and asked for money.

"I'm training for the Olympics," he told the crowd. "I will represent Cuba in the marathon. Please help me."

Felix kept appearing in the square, running lap after lap, and eventually gained enough money for his trip to St Louis. He gave up his job and bought a boat ticket to New Orleans, a southern American port. The boat journey passed smoothly, but unfortunately, when he reached New Orleans, he lost the rest of his money by gambling. He was left penniless in a foreign country, 700 miles (1120 km) from where the Olympic Games were being held. Yet Felix was determined to reach St Louis and run the marathon. He was very, very determined.

He was so determined, in fact, that he decided to run to the Olympics. He ran and ran and ran, and when he was too exhausted to run further he hitched rides in cars. He survived by begging food from farmhouses along the way and by picking fruit from the orchards at the roadside. He had little sleep or rest. He ran a grim race against the clock before the Games had even started, and finally arrived just in time for the marathon.

The other athletes in St Louis had heard vague rumours that a Cuban postman was travelling from New Orleans to join them for the race. They soon warmed to the tiny Cuban, and were amused by his appearance. Felix Carvajal lined up at the start of the race wearing heavy street shoes, long trousers and a long-sleeved shirt that was buttoned at his wrists. On his head was a beret. He was five feet tall and already dishevelled and weary after his long journey. He looked as likely to complete the course as the man holding the starting pistol.

A discus thrower called Martin Sheridan took pity on the Cuban. The start of the marathon was delayed while Sheridan found a pair of scissors and cut off the Cuban's trousers at the knees. Felix now looked a little more like an athlete, but he had never run a marathon before. In fact, Felix Carvajal had never run a competitive race of any kind.

So, on a scorching hot day 31 runners lined up to start the 1904 Olympic marathon. What a motley crew they were, dressed in all kinds of clothes. Most of them didn't know what to expect along the way. It was an unknown journey of 42 kilometres.

Felix Carvajal wasn't the only unusual competitor. Two African tribesmen, Lentauw and Yamasani, were in St Louis as part of the Boer War exhibition at the Louisiana Purchase Exposition. They thought they would wander along to give the marathon a try. They were the first black Africans to compete at the Olympics.

Most of the other entrants were either Americans or Greeks. The 16 Americans included three previous winners of the Boston Marathon – Sam Mellor, John Lordon and Michael Spring. The winner was expected to come from this trio. The ten Greeks had arrived from various parts of the States, and some of them had endured journeys as harrowing as that of Felix Carvajal.

In 1904 the modern Olympic Games were still in their infancy. This was only the third time the Games had been held. The words of Baron de Coubertin, founder of the Games, were still fresh in everyone's minds: "It is not the winning but the taking part, not the conquering but the playing fair." If anybody demonstrated the truth behind those words it was the Zulus, the Greeks and the Cuban postman. It seemed to many people watching that they were only there to make up the numbers.

In those days, of course, the world was very different from today. Transport was a real problem and the arrangements for the Olympics were not as sophisticated as they are now. The St Louis Games took place over several months. It was chaos at times. The organizers made mistakes. The competitors made mistakes. In the marathon almost everything went wrong.

The start went smoothly enough – the runners ran five laps of the stadium. When they left the stadium and ran on the open road the American Thomas Hicks was in the lead. Red

flags were stationed along the road so that the runners knew which route they had to follow. Behind them, on the ordinary roads around St Louis, came officials, doctors and journalists, all riding in automobiles. Unfortunately the effect of these early automobiles on the unmade roads of the 1900s was to send clouds of dust over the competitors. Every time a vehicle went past, the athletes were almost choked by the dust.

The race was run at a difficult time of day. When they set off, at 3.03 pm, the temperature was 90°F (32°C) and there was very little water available for the competitors.

After five kilometres Michael Spring had the lead and already 14 minutes separated the first runner from the last (the African Yamasani).

It was very hard on the runners. John Lordon, one of the favourites, was sick after 16 kilometres and had to withdraw from the race. Then William Garcia was found unconscious at the roadside. He had to be rushed to hospital where he nearly died. Michael Spring was also ill and had to be looked after in one of the motor cars. Fred Lorz, another early leader, and one of the best American runners, collapsed with leg cramps after 16 kilometres. Lorz was driven back towards the stadium.

Sam Mellor was now in the lead, but he was overcome by the conditions after 25 kilometres and he withdrew from the race. That left Thomas Hicks out in front. Hicks had a comfortable lead — over a mile — but he was also in trouble from the heat. He was tired. His legs hurt. He was hungry. He was thirsty. He wanted to lie down. He wanted to stop and rest. But his supporters urged him on and somehow Hicks kept going.

Lentauw, one of the Zulus, faced a different problem when he was chased off the course by two large dogs. After running into a cornfield to escape the dogs, Lentauw had to run back and pick up the route that he was supposed to have taken. This incident took him about a mile out of his way, and it cost him a lot of time. Other than that he was making good progress.

The officials were in trouble too. One of their cars swerved to avoid a runner and toppled down a steep embankment. Two officials were seriously injured.

And what about Felix Carvajal, the postman from Cuba who had given up his job and run 700 miles to St Louis? Well, despite the heat and the dust and the hills and all the other obstacles, Felix Carvajal was among the leaders. He stopped to chat to some of the cheering spectators and practised his broken English. He quenched his thirst by snatching peaches from an official in one of the cars. He was enjoying being part of the race.

Fred Lorz, meanwhile, riding along in the automobile, found that his leg cramps had eased. When the car broke down ten kilometres from the finish, Lorz got out and started running again. In front of him was Thomas Hicks, who was ashen-faced and barely moving. Lorz caught up with him and streaked past.

Felix Carvajal stopped and took some green apples from an orchard. He ate them as he ran. It was a mistake. He was soon suffering from stomach cramps.

Back in the stadium, the spectators were wondering what had happened to the runners. Over three hours had passed. Surely they couldn't be taking this long. The 1896 marathon

had been won in two hours and 55 minutes.

In the heat and the dust, the St Louis marathon was proving an exceptionally slow race. Most of the runners stopped and walked at some point. Some simply stopped. Only 14 were left in the race.

Three kilometres from the end, Hicks faced a steep hill. He slowed to a walk. It was the first time he had stopped running. At the top of the hill the crowd cheered him and he picked up the pace once more.

Finally, after more than three hours, a runner appeared in the stadium and the crowd cheered. But it wasn't Thomas Hicks, the leader; it was Fred Lorz, who had been ferried in a motor car for part of the way. The crowd thought they were cheering the winner, but they were cheering the wrong man. Lorz thought it would be a good joke to continue his run into the stadium.

The crowd didn't know what had happened on the roads. They cheered Lorz and marvelled at how fresh he looked. Lorz ran the statutory final lap of the stadium and across the finishing line.

The crowd hailed him as the winner.

Lorz was photographed with Alice Roosevelt, the daughter of the United States President, and officials prepared to award him the gold medal. For 15 minutes Fred Lorz was regarded by everyone in the stadium as the winner of the 1904 marathon. Then Thomas Hicks staggered into the arena.

Officials out on the course knew that Hicks was the leader. They were appalled by what Lorz had done.

Thomas Hicks won the race with six minutes to spare over the second-placed runner, Albert Corey of France. Another

13 minutes went by before Arthur Newton of America came in third.

After his win, Thomas Hicks was exhausted. His weight had dropped by 4.5 kilograms during the race. He was ready to retire from all long distance running. He had had enough.

"I would rather have won this race than be President of the United States," he told reporters.

And then the fourth-placed runner came across the finishing line. It was the heroic Cuban postman, Felix Carvajal. Everyone wondered where he might have finished if he had had better coaching, better diet, better preparation and an understanding of how to pace himself. Felix deserved a medal for simply being there. The courageous Cuban seemed to embody the very spirit of the Games.

• Lentauw, the black African runner, recovered from the incident with the dog to finish ninth.

• The Amateur Athletic Union officials banned Fred Lorz for life after his deception in the 1904 marathon. Lorz argued that he hadn't meant to hoodwink anybody; he had simply been overwhelmed by the reception when he entered the stadium. The ban was lifted and Lorz competed in the 1905 Boston marathon. He was so determined to do well that he literally ran himself into the ground. His feet were blistered and bleeding, but he won the race.

• Times for marathons have shown remarkable progress. Thomas Hicks won the 1904 marathon with a time of three hours and 28 minutes, whereas Young-Cho Hwang of South

Korea won the 1992 Olympic marathon in two hours and 13 minutes. In the same year Valentina Yegorova won the women's marathon in two hours and 32 minutes.

Long Distance Running

1. The 1908 Olympics produced another memorable marathon. Dorando Pietri, an Italian waiter, was first into the stadium with five minutes to spare over his nearest rival, the American John Hayes. Pietri stumbled a few yards and then collapsed but struggled on. Thirty metres from the finish officials helped Pietri to his feet and over the finishing line. The Italian, who was carried away on a stretcher, was later disqualified for receiving help, and Hayes was declared the winner. When Pietri recovered, Queen Alexandra personally awarded him a gold cup.

2. The 10,000 metres cross-country at the 1924 Olympics was incredibly demanding because of the hot weather. Thirty-nine runners started the race, but only 15 finished. Several collapsed in the stadium on the final lap and one started walking in the wrong direction when he was only 30 metres from the finish. The race was won by Paavi Nurmi, a Finnish runner, who had already won the 1,500 metres and 5,000 metres that week. Now Nurmi took gold for the team and individual cross-country, and later in the same week he won his fifth gold medal of the 1924 Olympics in the 3,000 metres team event. Altogether, Nurmi won nine Olympic gold medals and three silver medals.

3. Volmari Iso-Hollo of Finland won the gold in the 3,000 metres steeplechase at the 1932 Olympics. But there was a lot of confusion about second and third places, because an error by race officials meant that the runners had all run one lap too many. Joseph McCluskey of the USA was overtaken by the British runner Thomas Evenson during the extra lap, so even though Evenson came in second, he was really third. Or was he?

4. The 1954 Empire Games were held in Vancouver, Canada. At that time the marathon world record was held by Englishman Jim Peters. On a sweltering hot day Peters entered the Vancouver stadium with an astonishing lead of

about three miles. But at this stage in the race his legs were like rubber. He stumbled around the stadium, falling repeatedly and reached what he thought was the finishing line before collapsing once more. When he came round in hospital he learned that he had been 200 metres short of the actual line and hadn't finished the race.

5. In 1984, in the inaugural women's marathon, Gabriele Andersen-Scheiss entered the stadium and staggered an exceedingly slow and painful lap. It took her 5 minutes and 44 seconds to reach the finish in thirty-seventh place. Now runners are allowed to receive medical attention without fear of being disqualified.

FACT FILE • FACT FILE • FACT FILE • FACT FILE •

HORSE RACING

Devon Loch's Shock Finish

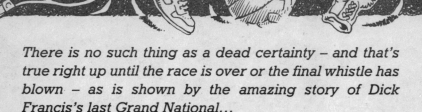

There is no such thing as a dead certainty – and that's true right up until the race is over or the final whistle has blown – as is shown by the amazing story of Dick Francis's last Grand National...

Aintree, Liverpool, 24 March 1956

National Hunt jockeys dream of winning the Grand National and Dick Francis was no exception. Towards the end of his riding career, he was still dreaming. Then, in 1956, he was given his best-ever chance. He would ride a good horse called Devon Loch. The race changed the jockey's life.

Dick Francis had been riding since he was five years old, when he first mounted a donkey and rode it without a saddle. As a child, he spent most of his spare time at gymkhanas and horse shows. By the time he was 16 his bedroom wall was full of rosettes and he was ready for point-to-point racing. He soon progressed to bigger races, and did well at them. Dick Francis was Champion Jockey in 1954. In fact he had done everything he wanted to do ... except win the Grand National. Then along came Devon Loch.

Devon Loch was a royal horse. He was owned by the Queen Mother, whose daughters, Queen Elizabeth and Princess Margaret, followed the horse with great interest. The British people were also fascinated. There hadn't been a royal victory in the Grand National since Ambush won in 1900, but Devon Loch had a good chance of changing that.

Three weeks before the Grand National, Dick Francis rode Devon Loch at Cheltenham in the National Hurdle. Although the horse finished only third, Francis was much encouraged

because he expected the horse to perform better at Aintree – the Grand National course was longer than the National Hurdle course at Cheltenham – and he knew that the horse was not yet at his best for the season.

Devon Loch was certainly an excellent horse. He started races slowly but stayed the course exceptionally well and jumped superbly. He was a big brown horse with a white mark on his forehead. He was as intelligent as he looked.

The horse showed his intelligence at Aintree on Grand National day. Dick Francis could not have dreamed of a better ride. Devon Loch sailed over the huge fences as if they were hurdles. The jockey wanted to hold him back on the first circuit, but the horse was happy to tuck in behind the leading pack.

The horse loved the race. Devon Loch leapt over the famous fences ... the sixth fence, known as Becher's Brook ... the eighth, the Canal Turn ... Valentine's Brook ... on and on, fence after fence.

There were 29 runners, and one by one they fell away. Four fell at the first fence, a difficult one which horses often took too fast because of the long approach. One fell at the third, another at the fourth. And so it went on, until there were only 16 horses left in the race and three fences to jump.

Devon Loch came alongside the leaders even though Francis was still holding the horse back. Horse and jockey were working well together – a winning team. Francis felt secure. He looked across and saw that the other jockeys were having to work hard on their mounts. He was convinced then that he was going to win.

Devon Loch was going clear as he met the last fence. He

timed his jump beautifully, cleared the fence and landed perfectly. Devon Loch was a couple of lengths clear and going for home. Despite such a long race, the horse seemed fresh and fast, and his rhythm was good.

The run-in to the finishing post is a long one for the Grand National. It didn't bother Devon Loch. The horse was simply pulling further away from second-placed ESB. Five lengths … six … seven … eight … nine … ten. Dick Francis and Devon Loch were alone on the course, ten lengths in the lead, finishing at a good pace, on course for a record time. In Lord Sefton's box, the royal party smiled and cheered. As Devon Loch came closer to victory, men raised their hats and stood to wave the horse home.

The finishing-post was less than 100 metres away now and Francis felt certain that he was going to win the National. His ambition would be achieved. The crowd cheered and Francis was joyful and triumphant. The race was Devon Loch's. Number five was coming home to win for the Queen Mother.

And then it happened.

The cheering stopped.

The crowd gasped.

It was an astonishing incident and it happened only 50 metres from the finish. One moment Devon Loch was galloping towards victory. The next he was out of the race. The horse's ears pricked and his hind legs went rigid. His legs splayed out sideways and backwards and the horse flopped on his belly.

The sudden stop jerked Dick Francis's right arm upwards, but he hung on as best he could with his left hand. He was left holding on to the horse's neck. A lesser jockey would have

fallen off.

ESB passed the stationary Devon Loch and went on to win the 1956 Grand National.

Devon Loch stood up and could hardly move. Then he started to walk perfectly normally.

Dick Francis was dazed and miserable. He threw his whip away in anger.

Devon Loch was out of the race.

The dream was over.

• People have always wondered what happened to Devon Loch in the 1956 Grand National. Was it a heart attack? Sudden cramp? Was the horse frightened by the noise of the cheering crowd? Only Devon Loch would ever know the real reason.

• Devon Loch later won races at Nottingham and Sandown Park. He also came second in the George VI Stakes. Devon Loch lived until 1963, to the ripe old age of 17.

• Other horses have stopped near the finishing line when looking certain to win a race. In one case a horse stopped so close to the finishing line that the judges had a hard time deciding whether he had finished first or last!

• Dick Francis retired soon after the 1956 Grand National and wrote his autobiography, *The Sport of Queens.* In it he described what it was like to ride Devon Loch. He went on to write thrillers set in the horse-racing world, and Dick Francis is now one of the world's best-selling authors.

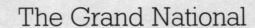

The Grand National

1. The most famous horse race of recent times is the 1993 Grand National ... because it never happened. To begin with the starter called back the 39 horses after a false start. A few minutes later he tried again. When he raised the starting-tape it became entangled with some of the horses and jockeys. The starter signalled a second false start by holding up his red flag. This time his flag did not unfurl, and the recall man didn't wave his flag in response. Thirty horses raced towards the first fence, thinking it was a real race. Some jockeys eventually realized what was happening, but seven horses completed the full course. The race was declared void, but like Dick Francis, John White, riding Esha Ness, approached the finishing line thinking he was going to win.

2. In 1849 the starter called a false start in the National but the spectators urged the jockeys to continue. The starter put down his flag and let them get on with it.

3. Red Rum must be the most famous horse ever to race in the Grand National, and his amazing record may never be beaten. In successive years, between 1973 and 1977, the horse finished first, first, second, second and first. When the 12-year-old horse galloped home for his third victory, the

noise from the cheering crowd was the loudest ever heard on a racecourse.

4. The 1993 Grand National was delayed at first by a group of animal rights demonstrators. They rushed on to the course, and unfurled a large banner saying "Stop the Slaughter" before the police caught up with them. They were protesting against the cruel treatment of horses in racing, particularly in the Grand National where the very difficult fences often mean that horses are killed or injured.

5. Protestors have interfered with other races. During the 1913 Epsom Derby, Emily Davison, an active "votes for women" campaigner, ran across the track in front of a horse owned by King George V. The galloping horse struck Emily Davison on the head and she died four days later.

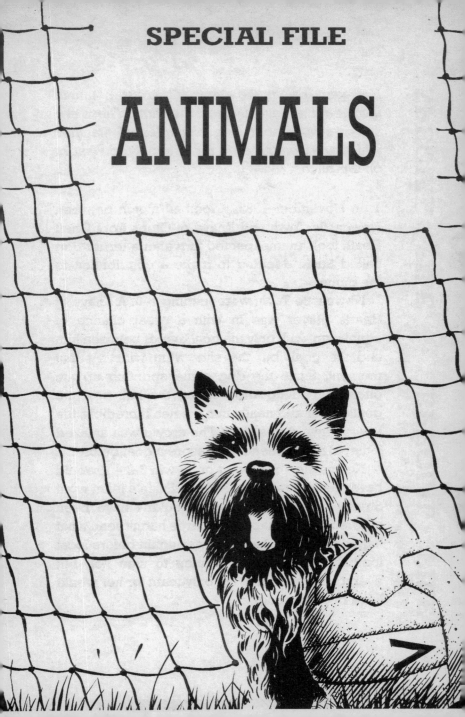

SPECIAL FILE

ANIMALS

However serious the event, if there's an animal involved it will usually steal the show! These are a few strange but true examples of matches which are remembered for unexpected visitors on the pitch.

1. In November 1985, a football match between Newcastle Town and Knave of Clubs from Chell Heath took an unexpected turn after a terrier dog called Susie decided to make a contribution to the game.

Newcastle Town were leading 1–0. A Knave of Hearts player was in with a great chance of equalizing, with only the goalkeeper between him and the goal, but the shot went wide. At that moment, Susie the dog came sprinting up the pitch, leaped up and headed the ball past the goalkeeper and neatly into the net. Incredibly, the referee awarded a goal! The crowd was amazed – they'd never seen a dog score a goal before.

Newcastle Town went on to win 3-2 – it would have seemed rather unfair had Susie's team won! Strictly speaking the goal shouldn't have been allowed, but perhaps the referee hadn't seen what happened. Susie had run away again before local football scouts had a chance to sign her, but everyone agreed that the only team for her would have been Barking!

SPECIAL FILE • SPECIAL FILE •

2. Fans at another local football match that same day witnessed a very strange sight when one of the goalkeepers was put off his game by a confused jackdaw. The bird continually flapped around him trying to perch on his head!

3. A cricket match in Oxford in 1962 was disrupted by a swarm of bees. Players from both teams fled from the pitch pursued by the swarm and took refuge in the cricket pavilion. They hid there until a beekeeper could be summoned.

4. A different kind of insect descended upon a Surrey cricket match in 1935. Flying ants made such a nuisance of themselves that the players were forced to abandon play while they set about the ants with stumps and bats. It was half an hour before the match could be resumed.

5. Two Canadian golfers were alarmed by a loud crashing noise during a quiet round of golf in Alberta, Canada, in 1925. They looked up to find a herd of 75 elk stampeding across the fairway! Petrified, the golfers watched as a male elk detached himself from the herd to make a charge at them. They managed to escape by clambering up a tree until the incensed elk got fed up and went away.

6. During the cycling world championships in 1928, Jules Van Hevel of Belgium was sharing the

lead with another competitor. The much-coveted world championship seemed within his grasp at last – until he collided with a cow and fell off his bike!

7. When the Birmingham City soccer team played Barnsley in March 1994, they were heading towards relegation from the First Division. The match was interrupted by the appearance of a stray dog, which ran rings round the players who were trying to catch him. City fans, disillusioned with their side's performance, chanted for the manager to sign on the dog!

TENNIS

The Tennis Marathon

When two evenly matched opponents are pitted against one another the match is usually an exciting one. An incredible Wimbledon tennis match between Gonzales and Pasarell turned out to be one of the most breath-takingly close-run of all time...

Wimbledon, London, Tuesday 24 and Wednesday 25 June 1969

In the first round of the Wimbledon tournament, Pancho Gonzales, a 41-year-old grandfather, played Charlie Pasarell, an American 16 years his junior. It was one of the all-time epic tennis matches.

The match was delayed for more than a day because of rain. Spectators sat under umbrellas and waited for play to start in what they knew would be a great match.

Finally, early on Tuesday evening, Pancho Gonzales and Charlie Pasarell walked on to Centre Court to start their match. The two players looked very different. On one side of the net was the young Pasarell, strong and powerful, splay-footed and ungainly, walking with a swagger. On the other side of the net, the ageing Gonzales, an aggressive, temperamental star, blessed with great strength but also a deftness of touch. His style had some similarities with that of contemporary hero André Agassi, a relative of Gonzales' by marriage.

Pasarell's parents had both been tennis champions in their native Puerto Rico. After winning five junior championships, including the United States under-18 championship in 1961, Pasarell had quickly made his mark at senior level by reaching

the United States singles quarter-finals in 1965 and then by achieving a sensational victory at Wimbledon two years later. When he beat Manuel Santana, Pasarell became the first player to knock out a reigning Wimbledon champion in a first-round match. Charlie Pasarell was certainly a rising star.

In contrast, Pancho Gonzales, his hair streaked with grey, was old enough, at 41, to be Pasarell's father. His full name was Ricardo Alonzo Gonzales but almost everyone called him Pancho. Throughout the 1950s he was the best tennis player in the world, but, because he was a professional, he was excluded from playing at Wimbledon. By the time the barriers were finally lifted, and Wimbledon was open to amateurs and professionals, Gonzales was well past his best.

Pasarell versus Gonzales was therefore a classic tennis encounter – the up-and-coming young player, Pasarell, against the older, experienced Gonzales.

The first set went with serve. Whenever Pasarell won his serve, Gonzales held his. Both players served powerfully.

One-one … two-two … three-three … four-four … five-five … six-six.

In those days there were no tie-breaks at six-all. Play went on and on. At twelve-all there was still no break of serve.

Then came a chance for Charlie Pasarell. He led 13-12 and had a point to win the set on the Gonzales serve. The point was saved.

Pasarell had two more set points at 15-14. And again Pancho Gonzales saved the set.

At 18-17 Pasarell had two further set points. Pancho Gonzales still held him off.

It went on and on.

When the score reached 20-all, there was a problem with the Centre Court scoreboard. In those days the numbers stopped at 20, so the scores were returned to nought. After more than 100 minutes of play, the scoreboard read love-all. They were back to the start.

At 21-20 to Pasarell, Pancho Gonzales faced three more set points. Incredibly he saved them all.

The crowd were now densely packed around Centre Court. They were wedged so closely together in the standing section that they had to clap with their hands above their heads.

Finally, in the forty-sixth game, the set was decided. Charlie Pasarell won his twelfth set point. This time his cunning lob eluded Pancho Gonzales and the ball landed on the line.

"First set to Pasarell, 24-22."

It was now eight o'clock on a dull summer's day. Pancho Gonzales complained about the light.

"Play on," said the umpire.

Gonzales was furious. He lost his concentration and played badly. He appealed against the light once more. He was turned down again.

Pasarell soon led four-one in the second set, and Pancho Gonzales was beside himself with rage. He shouted and threw his racket at the bottom of the umpire's chair and kicked it. He was booed by the crowd.

Although some spectators sympathized with him over the bad light, they realized that this was no way to react. His anger had gone too far. He appealed against the light for the third time but his appeal was turned down again. His temper got worse.

"You can't see a ball," he shouted at the umpire.

"Play on."

In the gloom of dusk, Gonzales lost the next two games.

"Second set to Pasarell," the umpire announced. "Six games to one. Pasarell leads by two sets to love."

Charlie Pasarell had the match in his grasp. He only needed one more set to win. At 8.15 that evening the match was finally abandoned for the day. Pancho Gonzales made no secret of his anger. As he left the court, he was jeered by the crowd.

That night Pancho told himself that it was a waste of energy to get upset. He had been stupid to let his mood affect his tennis. Now he had thrown away a set. He told himself to calm down. His pride was at stake.

The match continued at 2.42 the following afternoon. The conditions were almost perfect. It was a bright sunny day and there was a slight breeze to cool the players.

Charlie Pasarell and Pancho Gonzales resumed their battle. Their serves were just as powerful and the third set was as close as the first. A tired Pancho Gonzales was feeling his 41 years. He knew he needed to conserve his strength, and was careful to leave balls that he judged were going out of play. When he had to retrieve a ball he glided across the court and put all his strength and thought into his next shot. Most of all he remained calm. He waited patiently for his chance. Finally, it came. Pancho Gonzales broke the Pasarell serve in the thirtieth game and won the set 16-14.

Two sets to Pasarell, one to Gonzales.

Again, in the fourth set, Pancho Gonzales waited patiently for his chance to break Pasarell's serve. It came in the eighth game, when Charlie Pasarell served a double fault at 30-40.

Gonzales won the fourth set 6-3.

They now had two sets each.

The fifth set, predictably, went with serve. Pasarell served first. As the score reached five-four to Pasarell, the tension was mounting.

The next game started disastrously for Pancho Gonzales.

"Love-fifteen."

"Love-thirty."

"Love-forty."

Three match points to Pasarell.

Gonzales served. Charlie Pasarell returned. Gonzales hit the ball back and came to the net. Pasarell positioned himself to play the lob that would finish the match. All through the match he had tormented the older man with well-timed lobs that drifted over his head to win the point. Here was another winner.

Or was it?

The ball landed just beyond the line.

"Out."

"Fifteen-forty."

Gonzales served a winner.

"Thirty-forty."

He served again. Pasarell returned. Another rally. Another lob from Pasarell. Now he was getting nervous.

"Out."

"Deuce."

Pancho Gonzales had saved three match points. He went on to win the game.

"Five games all. Final set."

The spectators were on the edges of their seats. The next

crisis came two games later. Trailing five-six Gonzales was serving again at love-forty. He flashed a look of anguish around the court. His fans could hardly bear the tension.

A confident smash made the score 15-40.

A beautifully-timed forehand across court made it 30-40.

A winning serve saved the third match point.

Gonzales went on to win the game.

"Six games all. Final set."

Fifteen hundred spectators were spellbound. They had never seen such a struggle. Then came another problem for Pancho Gonzales. He was getting cramp on the inside of his thigh.

At eight-seven in the final set, Charlie Pasarell had his seventh match point. He hit another lob. Pancho Gonzales forced his tired legs into action and sprinted after the ball. It was out of his range, but the ball drifted inches out of court. Gonzales went on to hold his serve.

"Eight games all. Final set."

The next two games went with serve.

Gonzales' nerves were stretched. He flicked sweat from his forehead. He hitched his sodden shirt back on to his shoulders.

On Pasarell's next serve, he saw his chance.

"Love-fifteen."

"Love-thirty."

Now Pancho Gonzales sensed that the younger man was nervous and tense. He forgot the cramp in his thigh. He threw everything into the next two points and broke Charlie Pasarell's serve.

"Gonzales leads ten games to nine. Final set. Two sets all."

For the first time in the match Pancho Gonzales had an overall lead. He doused himself with water.

As Gonzales walked back on the court he vowed to hold his serve. He bounced the ball in front of him, threw it up and served.

The point was his.

And the next.

And another.

"Forty-love."

Now, after five hours and 12 minutes, Pancho Gonzales had his first match point.

He threw the ball into the air, served and put all his effort and determination into his play. The point was his.

"Game, set and match to Gonzales. 22-24, 1-6, 16-14, 6-3, 11-9."

And so ended an incredible match. They had played 112 games in 312 minutes. They had used 13 sets of balls.

The crowd cheered and cheered. The previous day they had booed Pancho Gonzales off the court. Now, as he limped away, they hailed him as their hero.

• The Gonzales-Pasarell match broke Wimbledon long-match records in terms of time and number of games.

• The first set of the Gonzales-Pasarell match equalled the longest set at Wimbledon for a singles match. In the doubles, however, Wimbledon has seen a 62-game set, won 32-30 by Olmedo and Segura against Forbes and Segal.

• The record for the most games in a set and the most games

in a match belong to a 1967 three-set doubles match. Dell and Leach beat Mozur and Schloss 3-6, 49-47, 22-20. (Good job it wasn't a five-set match!)

• Tennis professionals were banned from major championships until December 1967, when it was announced that there was to be no distinction between amateurs and professionals. Since then all competitors have been known as "players". So in 1968 Pancho Gonzales was able to play as a professional for the first time.

• In 1969 after Gonzales had beaten Pasarell in the epic match on Centre Court, he won two more matches that same week. He beat Bengtson in three sets and Edelfsen in three sets, before losing to Arthur Ashe in four sets in the fourth round. Many people still say that Pancho Gonzales was probably the best player never to win Wimbledon.

Tie Breaks

1. In 1971 a 12-point tie-break rule was introduced to Wimbledon. But at first tie-breaks did not decide the final set of a match. Consequently, a 1982 match between John McEnroe and Mats Wilander lasted six hours and 32 minutes.

2. Even modern day tie-breaks can go on forever. In 1993 Goran Ivanisevic and Daniel Nestor played 38 points in a tie-break, as many as in some sets. Ivanisevic won the tie-break 20-18.

3. Other sports have had to find shortcuts to a definite result. In football the matter came to a head soon after the 1971 FA Cup qualifying round tie between Alvechurch and Oxford City. It took six games in 17 days to settle that Cup tie. Penalty shoot-outs were introduced, but these don't always have quick endings. The 1975 Asia Cup semi final between Hong Kong and North Korea ended 3-3 after extra-time, so each team took five penalties. That finished 4-4, so they carried on with sudden-death penalties. North Korea eventually won the shoot-out 11-10 on the twenty-eighth penalty!

4. Horse race judges faced major problems in the days before photo-finish cameras. The naked eye was not always quick enough to pick out the

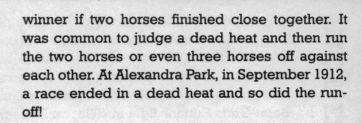

winner if two horses finished close together. It was common to judge a dead heat and then run the two horses or even three horses off against each other. At Alexandra Park, in September 1912, a race ended in a dead heat and so did the run-off!

5. In 1893, two boxers, Andy Bowen and Jack Burke, fought for seven hours and 19 minutes because they had agreed to fight to a finish. At the end of the one hundred and tenth round they were both exhausted. Their eyes were puffed and their

arms were swollen from stopping each other's blows. The referee stopped the fight and called it a draw. Later judges were introduced so that boxers could win or lose on a point system after a set number of rounds. But fights, such as the Nigel Benn-Chris Eubank fight in 1993, can still end in a draw.

6. Even the Oxford-Cambridge boat race has gone to a replay. It happened in 1912. The race started in rough water. The Cambridge boat soon ran into trouble and eventually sank. The crew had to swim ashore. Oxford had only to finish the race to win, but they sank in rough water near Hammersmith Bridge. The umpire declared it "no race". Oxford won the re-row the following Monday.

7. The 1994 soccer World Cup Final between Italy and Brazil was a goalless draw after extra time. Millions of fans watching the match on television were amazed when the result was finally decided with a penalty shoot-out. Brazil won the Cup, but fans of both teams were disappointed that such an important match should be decided in this way.

BOXING

"I am the Greatest"

When Cassius Clay, a young unknown boxer, challenged the World Heavyweight Champion Sonny Liston, few people believed he could win. But Clay knew he could and he didn't hesitate to tell the world...

Miami, Florida, USA, 25 February 1964

> Clay comes out to meet Liston
> And Liston starts to retreat
> If Liston goes back any further
> He'll end up in a ringside seat.

Cassius Marcellus Clay, a tall, handsome, witty 22-year-old, was about to fight Sonny Liston for the World Heavyweight Championship. Clay appeared to have little chance of winning the title. He was too young and too inexperienced. And Liston, the champion, was a ferocious and frightening fighter.

The stories about Sonny Liston were terrifying. It was rumoured that he was one of 25 children and left home at the age of 13 to take up with a bad crowd. He had been arrested a hundred times. He'd been to prison for armed robbery. When he was released, he went back to prison for assaulting a policeman. It was in prison that he took up boxing and he then went on to box professionally. But he still had a reputation for associating with some very shady characters.

One thing was certain though – Sonny Liston was a great boxer and worthy champion. He had won the World Heavyweight crown by knocking out Floyd Patterson in the first round of their title fight. In a return fight, Patterson had again been floored by a first-round knockout. It was very convincing

boxing from Liston, who had not lost for ten years.

It wasn't only his background and fighting record that made Liston formidable. There was also something about the way he looked. He was as big as a bear and his expression was permanently sullen. His thin moustache increased his surly appearance. Yes, Sonny Liston looked big and mean.

In contrast to Liston, Cassius Clay was a novice. This was only Clay's twentieth professional fight. No wonder all the betting favoured Liston, and 43 out of 46 newspaper experts predicted that Liston would win. The only question was, "in which round?"

Unlike Liston, Cassius Clay didn't look like a boxer. He had the looks and charisma of a film star. He didn't carry any scars from his fights, and he was very aware that he was handsome. If anybody hadn't heard of him, they soon would, because Cassius Clay would tell them. He was known as the Mighty Mouth, or Louisville Lip (because Louisville was his home town). He couldn't stop talking about how good he was and how pretty he was. He even made up poems about himself and forthcoming fights:

It all started twenty years past
The greatest of them all was born at last.
The very first words from his Louisville lips,
"I'm pretty as a picture, and there's no one I can't whip."

Cassius Clay made predictions about when his fights would end, and many of them came true. "Besmanof must fall in seven," he told reporters, and lo and behold, Besmanof was knocked out in the seventh round. He said he would knock out

Sonny Banks in the fourth and he did. Then he predicted what would happen to Archie Moore: "When you come to the fight, don't block the aisle and don't block the door. You will all go home after round four."

Experienced boxing observers were not taken in by Clay's bravado. "It's all very well to boast when he's just starting his career and he's fought against easy opponents," they said about Clay. "This loud mouth from Louisville will soon be cut down to size. Wait until he gets in the same ring as Sonny Liston."

It didn't stop the Louisville Lip from speaking out. He called Liston "a big ugly bear" and appeared in public with a bear-trap. "He's too ugly to be world champion," Clay taunted. He told everyone that he dreamed of building himself a pretty home and using Liston as a bearskin rug.

It was unusual then for boxers to promote a fight with outspoken remarks. Weigh-ins, on the day of the fight, were usually polite and quiet. But the Liston-Clay weigh-in set the pattern for the future. It was an amazing scene.

Clay appeared at the weigh-in wearing a blue denim jacket. On the back of the jacket the words "Bear Huntin'" were embroidered in red. Clay was shouting: "Float like a butterfly, sting like a bee ... float like a butterfly, sting like a bee." He was hysterical. He was out of control. He was shouting and heckling like a crazy man, telling everyone that he was already the champion. He ranted and raved. He was ready to fight there and then. He had to be held back from doing just that.

Nobody knew what to make of it. Was he scared to death? Was he mad? Was it all an act – a way of publicizing himself? Or was it simply his way of unsettling Sonny Liston, who

certainly couldn't work out what was happening?

When the fight came it was one of the most dramatic in the history of boxing. When the referee called them together, Sonny Liston and Cassius Clay stared menacingly at each other. Both boxers were more nervous than usual. Clay knew there was no turning back, he had to go through with the fight. Liston didn't know what to expect from his half-crazed opponent.

In the first round Liston couldn't catch up with the faster Clay, who danced around the ring, holding his hands low, ducking and dodging, and bobbing his head. Liston couldn't land his powerful jab because Clay was dancing like a flyweight. For the first time, the people in Liston's corner thought that their boxer might have some trouble with the challenger. When the bell sounded for the first round Clay had won on points.

Liston did better in the second round and began to catch Clay with his wicked left hooks. Clay was dancing out of trouble, but he needed to. Liston chased him and took the initiative. That round went to Liston.

By the third round it was obvious that Liston was tiring a little. Clay decided to test him. He hit Liston once, twice, then again and again. A cut opened under Liston's left eye. Until then, Liston had seemed indestructible. But Liston fought back and hit Clay repeatedly towards the end of the round. Clay and Liston scored equal points.

Liston got well on top in the fourth round. Then near the end of the round Cassius Clay began to have trouble with his eyes. He couldn't see. His eyes were burning. At the end of the round there was real concern in his corner.

Clay's trainer cleaned the boxer's eyes and sent him back out. "This is the big one, daddy. Stay away from him. Run!"

Cassius Clay did his best to stay away from the world champion, but Liston was now well on top. Clay used his feet to dance around the ring and keep out of range as much as possible. The champion sensed that this was a chance to knock out Clay, but midway through that fifth round Clay's eyes cleared and he could see properly again.

The next round saw Clay back in charge. He stayed away from Liston's punches and then hit the champion when he wanted. The round went to Clay. When the bell rang they retired to their respective corners. The official scored the round. The fight was very close and what happened next changed the course of boxing.

Liston did not come out for the next round.

His eyes were cut, his face swollen and his shoulder hurt. He knew the fight was lost. He stayed on his stool defeated. The fight was over. Cassius Clay, the young upstart with the big mouth, was the champion of the world. He danced around the ring shouting: "I am the greatest! I am the greatest! I'm the greatest! I'm king of the world!"

• Although Cassius Clay had fought only 20 professional fights, by 1964, he had fought 116 fights as an amateur (108 wins) and had been 1960 Olympic Light-heavyweight Champion.

• The morning after Cassius Clay became Heavyweight Champion of the World he made it clear that he was committed to the religion of Islam. He changed his name from his "slave name" (Cassius Clay) to an Islamic name (Muhammad Ali). In one fight he mercilessly punished Ernie Terrell with punches while shouting, "What's my name?"

• When Muhammad Ali and Sonny Liston fought a return fight for the Championship, in Lewiston, Maine, Ali knocked out Liston in the first round.

• Muhammad Ali refused to serve in the United States army in Vietnam on religious grounds. "Man, I ain't got no quarrel with them Vietcong," he said. His World Heavyweight title was stripped from him in 1967, but his stance on the Vietnam War brought him as much fame and admiration as his boxing. Despite missing three years of boxing, Muhammad Ali came back to regain the World Heavyweight Championship, beating George Foreman in Zaire in October 1974.

• Ali had defended his title ten more times before he lost the Championship to Leon Spinks. He won it back again by beating Spinks in September 1978. Muhammad Ali was 36 years old when he won the title for the third time. He goes down in history as one of the finest boxers of all time, and certainly one of its most memorable characters.

• Muhammad Ali approached his 50th birthday suffering from Parkinson's Disease, one of a number of diseases that can be brought on by receiving too many punches in a boxing ring. Boxing officials have done their best to make boxing safer over the years but blows will always cause damage.

Boxing

1. Joe Louis held the World Heavyweight title longer than any other boxer. He was champion for 12 years from June 1937. During that time Louis successfully defended his title 25 times.

2. Sugar Ray Robinson regained the World Middleweight Championship four times. What made this even more amazing was that Robinson was over 31 years old when he first won the title in February 1951. Sugar Ray Robinson had also been World Welterweight Champion between 1946 and 1951.

3. Rocky Marciano, World Heavyweight Champion from 1952 to 1955, was undefeated during his professional boxing career. He won all his 49 fights. Many boxers have been nicknamed "Rocky", but the films of that name are not based on a real boxer.

4. It's not often that a boxer wins a fight after being knocked out! At the start of the second round of the fight between Jim Boyce and Len Gascoyne in 1940, both boxers rushed from their corner and, simultaneously, connected with terrific left hooks to the jaw. Both boxers were knocked out. The referee declared Boyce the winner because he had won the first round on points!

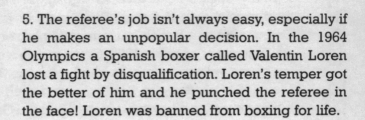

5. The referee's job isn't always easy, especially if he makes an unpopular decision. In the 1964 Olympics a Spanish boxer called Valentin Loren lost a fight by disqualification. Loren's temper got the better of him and he punched the referee in the face! Loren was banned from boxing for life.

6. During a 1991 super-middleweight fight, Michael Watson suffered serious brain damage and was in a coma for months. Eventually he regained his ability to communicate. Paralysed down the left side, he is now confined to a wheelchair.

7. Many boxers have died as a result of injuries they received in the ring. They include Johnny Owen, a gallant British bantamweight boxer who was injured in a fight in 1980. Owen was in a coma for seven weeks before he died. He was 24. In May 1994, 23-year-old Bradley Stone died after being injured in a boxing match in Bethnal Green, London. Because of these and similar accidents, many people believe boxing should be banned.

SPECIAL FILE

THE
WEATHER

Rain, fog, snow, extreme heat, electrical storms – the weather is a completely unpredictable element when a sports event is planned. Here are a few sports stories where the weather has played a surprising part.

1. In 1908, the England-Wales rugby union international had been carefully planned and was eagerly awaited by thousands of fans. But one important detail couldn't be planned – the British weather.

Despite the fog, the match went ahead as scheduled. But before long, no-one – not the crowd, the sports reporters, the referee or the players – could see enough to work out exactly what was going on. Visibility was so bad that the people had to guess whether a try had been scored and whether or not the conversion had been made. Reporters had to guess the score. In the second half, the fog was so bad that spectators couldn't see any of the players. Undeterred, the teams valiantly played on, looming out of the fog every so often to give the crowd a tantalizing glimpse of what might be happening. Visibility was down to three metres.

Only after a lot of discussion was the result known – Wales 28, England 18. Reporters had only actually seen one of the five tries.

2. A football match between Charlton Athletic and Chelsea in 1937 had to be abandoned because of

dense fog. The Charlton players were in the bath afterwards when someone noticed that the goal-keeper was missing. The poor goalie had been hopping about in the goal mouth for fifteen minutes after play had been abandoned before a policeman finally came and gave him the news.

3. Five Manchester City footballers fell sick with sunstroke during their match with Arsenal at the start of the season in 1906. City finished the game with only six players on the field. Despite a valiant effort by the remaining City players, Arsenal won!

4. "Rain stopped play" is not an uncommon announcement at British cricket games. But in *June* 1975, at the height of the British summer, a day's play was lost because it *snowed!*

5. It can be very dangerous to be on a golf course during a thunder storm. Lee Trevino was fortunate to survive an accident in 1975 when he was struck by lightning, and lifted half a metre into the air by the force of it. After a stay in hospital, he soon recovered his health and his sense of humour, wondering whether he might be penalized for slow play!

6. A horse race in 1889 was so badly affected by fog that all the horses went the wrong way and straight into a set of black hoardings at full racing speed. Amazingly, none of the jockeys or horses

was seriously injured. At a Cheltenham race meeting in 1841, the fog was so bad that the leading horse pulled up too early – the jockey thought he had passed the finishing line in the fog; he hadn't, and lost the race!

ATHLETICS

The Fastest
Women in the
World

The story of Wilma Rudolph, who became a world class athlete despite serious illness and even paralysis, is truly inspirational. Her British contemporary Dorothy Hyman didn't have an easy ride to the top of her sport either. Their backgrounds were very different, but these courageous young women were both driven by determination to excel at their sport...

Wilma Rudolph came from a big family. Her parents had eight children, and her father had another eleven by a previous marriage. The house was very full.

As an infant Wilma was often sick. She weighed only four and a half pounds at birth, and her parents were not sure if she would survive. In her early years she suffered with polio. At the age of four she went down with double pneumonia and scarlet fever. She was paralysed in her left leg. She couldn't stand. She couldn't walk. She certainly couldn't run.

The Rudolphs lived in a small town in Tennessee in the midwest of the United States. It was a poor area where tobacco and corn were grown. The family didn't have much money. When Wilma was ill, it was a real strain. The nearest special hospital was nearly 40 miles away. Once a week Wilma's mother picked up her child, wrapped her in a blanket and travelled by bus to the hospital. This went on for two years.

When Wilma was six she could hop around on one leg. She wore specially constructed shoes and a brace on her bad leg. Then her mother learned that the leg might improve with frequent massages. The family set to work. Wilma's leg was massaged four times a day. By the time she was eight she could walk.

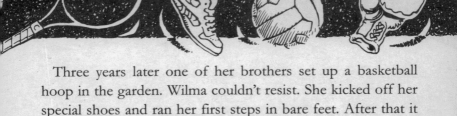

Three years later one of her brothers set up a basketball hoop in the garden. Wilma couldn't resist. She kicked off her special shoes and ran her first steps in bare feet. After that it was basketball, basketball, basketball.

She played basketball for her school, and they nicknamed her "Skeeter" because she buzzed around like a mosquito. Basketball took up all her time ... then she discovered athletics.

The basketball players began to practise sprints in order to improve their speed on the basketball court. Wilma Rudolph went further. By the time she was 16 she was a star runner. She qualified for the United States Olympic team and travelled to the 1956 Olympic Games in Melbourne, Australia. She didn't get past the first round of the 200 metres but her main chance came in the 4 x 100 metres relay. She ran the third leg. Her team finished third and she won a bronze medal. Pretty good for a schoolgirl who had been paralysed in one leg.

Dorothy Hyman grew up in the same era. Her family lived in a council house in South Yorkshire, England, and her father was a coal-miner.

Dorothy went to a local school. She declared her ambitions in a school essay when she was 13: "When I grow up to be a lady I would like to be a great runner ... perhaps an Olympic champion."

As a child she ran everywhere, until one day when she ran into a car! Luckily, she was unhurt but after that Dorothy tried to confine her running to fields and running tracks.

At 13 she was already competing against adults. That was when her father decided she needed a pair of proper running

shoes. Dorothy loved them, and trained even harder.

Dorothy went on to win county and national schools sprint championships, becoming a local celebrity.

After leaving school to work in a factory Dorothy continued with her running. Every night after work she trained in all kinds of weather. She even practised sprinting in the dark as there were no floodlit or indoor tracks. Once she ran right into a goalpost! Dorothy was determined and refused to let the lack of facilities put her off.

When she was 17, Dorothy ran in the Empire Games in Cardiff, as England's second runner in the 4 x 110 yards relay. She was thrilled to see her team come home first. Amazingly, they had run a world record time.

A few weeks before the 1960 Olympics, Dorothy's mother read out some news in an athletics magazine.

"An American girl has set a new world record for the 200 metres. Twenty-two point nine," she said.

"What's her name?" Dorothy asked.

"Wilma Rudolph. She won a bronze medal in the 1956 Olympics as a 16-year-old. In the relay."

But 22.9 seconds for the 200 metres?

Was it wind-assisted? Dorothy wondered. Or was it a fluke?

Dorothy Hyman would find out at the 1960 Olympics.

Rome, Italy, September 1960

Wilma Rudolph gave up athletics for much of 1958 because she was having a baby. She went to college on a sports scholarship and began a vigorous training programme. She had a happy-go-lucky approach to life. Having overcome her ill-

nesses, having struggled to learn to walk and then to run, she was just glad to be running. Nothing seemed impossible.

It showed in Rome, in 1960, when Wilma Rudolph made her mark on the Olympic Games.

In the semi-final of the 100 metres, Wilma Rudolph equalled the world record of 11.3 seconds.

The second 100 metres semi-final was won by Dorothy Hyman in 11.5 seconds, a new United Kingdom record.

At four o'clock in the afternoon, on a blazing hot September day, the two girls lined up next to each other for the final of the 100 metres. They were a contrasting pair.

Dorothy was a slim 5ft 7in with dark hair. She was pale-skinned and poker-faced. She looked serious. Inwardly she was tense and emotional. She was always worried about falling over or dropping the baton in relay races.

Wilma was by far the tallest girl in the race. She was 5ft 11in with long legs and a short torso. She had black skin and a chirpy disposition. She oozed confidence. There was a twinkle in her eye as if she were amused by something or surprised by the fuss.

The tension mounted as the athletes were kept waiting at the start because the crowd were cheering the end of the previous race. Eventually silence settled over the stadium. The gun went and they were off ... to a false start.

The six girls regrouped. The starting gun was fired again. This time they were away.

Wilma had a bad start but streaked away after 30 or 40 metres of the race. The crowd gasped in surprise as each long, raking stride took Wilma further into the lead. On her left, Dorothy kept her in her sight. Inspired by the occasion she ran her fastest yet to pip Giuseppe Leone of Italy for the silver medal.

The winning time was 11 seconds. It would have been a world record but for the following wind.

The two girls met again in the final of the 200 metres. Wilma had already created an Olympic record with a time of 23.2 seconds in her opening heat. Then she set a new world record in the next heat. She might have set another in the final but the conditions were poor. Rain soaked the track, and the wind hit the runners in the face as they came into the home straight. Wilma won in style, but Dorothy Hyman held on for third place and the bronze medal.

When the medals were presented, three girls climbed on to the rostrum. Gold medallist Wilma Rudolph came from a poor family in the United States and had overcome severe illness to reach the top. Silver medallist Jutta Heine was a 5ft 11in blonde, the daughter of a very rich German lawyer. And the bronze medallist Dorothy Hyman was the daughter of a Yorkshire coal-miner. Wilma Rudolph waved her straw hat in the air then put her arms around the other two medal winners.

If it hadn't been for athletics it is extremely unlikely that these girls would ever have met.

• Wilma Rudolph's achievement of three sprint gold medals was not unique. Fanny Blankers-Koen of Holland won four gold medals at the 1948 Olympic Games in London. Australian Betty Cuthbert won three gold medals at the 1956 Melbourne Olympics.

• In 1961 Wilma Rudolph set a new 100 metres record of 11.2

seconds, but she retired from athletics soon afterwards. Later she helped establish the Wilma Rudolph Foundation for work with underprivileged children.

• In 1962 Dorothy Hyman was 100 metres champion and 200 metres silver medallist at the European Games. That same year she was Commonwealth Games 100 yards and 220 yards champion.

• The Dorothy Hyman Centre was built in the athlete's honour in her native South Yorkshire. The area provided facilities for young athletes to train without some of the risks Dorothy Hyman had endured.

Winning against all odds

1. Gail Devers won the women's 100 metres gold medal at the 1992 Barcelona Olympics after facing an uphill struggle against illness. In 1988 she suffered severe weight loss and was diagnosed with Graves' Disease, a rare thyroid complaint. By 1991 she could hardly walk but then her treatment was changed and she was able to take up athletics training again. The gold medal was a miraculous outcome.

2. Pete Gray played major-league baseball for St Louis Browns in 1945. A fact made amazing because Gray had only one arm. He had lost his right arm in a boyhood accident.

3. National Hunt jockey Bob Champion was a 30-year-old cancer patient in 1979. After chemo-therapy treatment he was thin, wasted and had little strength in his muscles. He fought his way back courageously, and when he won the 1981 Grand National on Aldaniti it was one of sport's most popular victories.

4. Károly Takács was a member of Hungary's 1938 world-champion pistol-shooting team, and an army sergeant. Later that year, he was wounded by a grenade, which shattered his right hand, the one he used for shooting. Undeterred, Takács

taught himself to shoot with his left hand, and won gold medals for rapid-fire pistol shooting at the 1948 and 1952 Olympics.

5. Lis Hartel competed in the 1952 and 1956 Olympics and won a silver medal for dressage on each occasion. This was amazing because she was paralysed from the knees down. She contracted polio when she was a very promising 23-year-old horsewoman, but her determination had enabled her to walk with crutches and ride a horse again.

6. Disabled sport is now recognized on a world scale and the Paralympic Games and World Championships run in parallel to the able-bodied Olympics and World games.

The 1920s and 30s was the era of marathons in the USA. It was the time of the Great Depression and people organized and took part in these gruelling events in the hope of making money. Dance marathons are perhaps the most famous and were incredible tests of endurance, but most amazing of all was the punishing race across America that became known as the Bunion Derby...

Every day from 4 March to 26 May 1928
3,422 miles from Los Angeles to New York City, USA

Over two hundred men plodded through the mud at Ascot Speedway Stadium to complete the first mile of their long and arduous journey.

"Only another 3,421 miles to go!"

This was the first Transcontinental Marathon. Day after day, lap after lap, from town to town ... until they had completed 3,422 miles (5500 km) in 84 days and crossed the American continent. It was one of the greatest tests of endurance that was ever suffered in the name of sport. The race was soon called the Bunion Derby.

The event was organized by Charles C Pyle, a sports promoter. Pyle was the agent of two famous sports stars – Suzanne Lenglen, the first professional tennis player, and American football player "Red" Grange. Charles C Pyle owned a chain of shops; hence his nickname – "Cash and Carry" Pyle. Before the end of the Transcontinental Marathon, he was also known as "Corn and Callus" Pyle ... or even "Corn and Callous" Pyle.

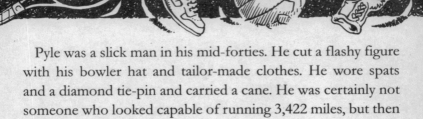

Pyle was a slick man in his mid-forties. He cut a flashy figure with his bowler hat and tailor-made clothes. He wore spats and a diamond tie-pin and carried a cane. He was certainly not someone who looked capable of running 3,422 miles, but then he left the running to others.

The runners each paid Pyle a $25 entry fee, and Pyle promised to finance all their food and accommodation on the journey. In return, there were prizes for the first runners across the finishing-line. The first prize of $25,000 attracted many of the entrants. Even the tenth prize of $1,000 was a great deal of money then. This was the depression, when many people were unemployed and desperate for money and food.

The runners came together for special training three weeks before the race. Some were runners of Olympic standard, others had great potential, but a few were there for the publicity alone. They were a mixed bunch. There was a 16-year-old boy and a grey-haired 63-year-old man. There was a boy with one arm, a man with a cane and a Hindu philosopher. There were also people like Arthur Newton, who had run Olympic marathons, and Nicholas Quomahwahu, a famous Hopi Indian runner. They would be running together day after day after day.

The first lap of the race was between Puente, a district of Los Angeles, and Bloomington. At 16 miles, this was the shortest lap of the race. The runners faced a strict midnight curfew or they were out of the race, and even this short lap brought problems for some. Approximately 275 runners started from Los Angeles and the winner of the first lap was Willie Kolehmainen, a Finnish runner, brother of the 1920

Olympic marathon champion. Another Finn, Gunnar Nilsen, was second. They both completed the course in 98 minutes. But remember the fable of the tortoise and the hare. Kolehmainen set off quickly but dropped out of the race on the fourth day's run to Barstow, California.

The first to show a clear overall lead was Quomahwahu, the American Indian runner, who took the lead on the rainy second day. Quomahwahu held the lead on the third day's 45-mile lap, when the runners climbed up long, steep mountainous slopes and across the windswept Californian desert. On the fourth day Quomahwahu was seized by cramps and reduced to a walk. He lost his lead, sprained his ankle on the seventh day and finally dropped out of the race on the thirteenth day.

Oli Wantinen, another Finn, was the third runner to hold the overall lead, but he was soon overtaken by 44-year-old Arthur Newton, the 100-mile running champion of England. For a week, in the desert, Newton was magnificent. He won lap after lap across the dusty, dirty roadways, coping with a blistering 90°F (32°C) sun and 40 miles-per-hour chilly winds, watched only by cactus plants. By the time they reached Peach Springs, Arizona, Arthur Newton had won six of the first eleven laps. His time for the first 397 miles was 61 hours and 23 minutes, and he had a clear lead. In fact, by day 14 Newton had a lead of nearly nine hours. Then he sprained his ankle near Flagstaff, Arizona, and was out of the race.

The lead was now with Andy Payne, a 19-year-old farmboy from Oklahoma who was part Cherokee Indian. But Payne was struck down by tonsillitis. Despite a fever, rather than quit he slowed to a walk and sacrificed several hours of his time.

He managed to make the midnight curfews necessary to stay in the race, but his lead was taken by Arne Souminen of Detroit.

By the twenty-fifth day, Souminen had a lead of three hours from a British runner, Peter Gavuzzi. Andy Payne had recovered his best form and was a well-placed third. These three runners had run 892 miles in less than 154 hours. It was a cracking pace. It took phenomenal stamina.

Only another 2,530 miles to go!

Ninety-two runners were left in the race. They were dropping out for all sorts of reasons. Seventy of the more ambitious runners had fallen away during the first two days, but some of the best runners were struck by unlucky injuries. About a dozen were hit by passing cars and put out of the race with broken ribs and broken legs. Some were left unconscious at the roadside as the rest plodded wearily on.

There were many other reasons for quitting — stomach trouble, blisters and bunions, homesickness, exhaustion and general breakdown. A few were thrown out of the race for hitching rides in passing cars. Many runners had sunburned skin, sore legs and badly damaged feet.

The remaining runners went on and on. They ran across the state of New Mexico and, on the thirty-second day, entered Texas. Souminen had increased his lead to over five hours but on the thirty-fifth day he pulled a tendon and was out of the race. Andy Payne, now fully recovered from tonsillitis, was back in the lead.

For the next week Payne retained a lead of just over two hours on his nearest rival Gavuzzi. Then Payne slipped down the field and, on day 43, Gavuzzi was the new race leader.

They ran through Payne's home state of Oklahoma. Cheering crowds welcomed him, and, at one point, about a thousand cars drove the route with the runners. Payne quickened his stride as he ran near to his home town. People pressed money into his hand, and, when he regained the lead from Gavuzzi, he had his eyes on the first prize again.

As they entered the state of Illinois, the lead passed to Peter Gavuzzi from Southampton, England. On day 56 he stepped up the pace and extended his lead to three hours. By now, third-placed John Salo trailed over 30 hours behind the two leaders.

Seventy-one determined, sunburned runners had survived the first 2,200 miles of the race. They were into the state of Indiana now, and Gavuzzi had increased his lead to more than six hours.

Then Gavuzzi had a problem. He was in severe pain from an infected tooth and had eaten nothing but liquid food. He became so weak that on the sixty-eighth day he had to drop out. He had run 2,654 miles for nothing.

Andy Payne once more had the lead; this time he was over 22 hours ahead of John Salo. Slowly, Salo clawed back the time and when they reached Deposit, New York, Andy Payne's lead was less than 16 hours. Andy wasn't worried. He was running his own race and there were only seven days to go.

John Salo slowed down because of trouble with his feet, but the drama was far from over. On the eighty-third day the race passed through John Salo's home town of Passaic, New Jersey. There were rumours that Andy Payne, the leader, might be attacked. Payne was given a police escort just in case.

Banners of welcome greeted John Salo in his home town,

and Salo won the lap.

The next day was the last of the race. A huge crowd turned out in New York City to see the runners. They were a sad sight: glassy-eyed, sunburned, weather-beaten, bandaged, bearded and emaciated. Some ran on their heels because their toes hurt while others ran on their toes because their heels hurt.

"Come on, you fellows," shouted Corn and Callous Pyle. "Streak it, boys, streak it. Show them what I've brought to New York."

The race ended with a 20-mile run in Madison Square Gardens. More drama was to come. Andy Payne was running automatically, his aching limbs going though mindless motion, and he ran into a concrete pillar only a few laps from the end. Fortunately, he recovered fairly quickly and jogged to the end of the race.

Payne was hailed as the winner of the longest foot-race of all time. When a doctor examined him, he said that Payne had knocked ten years off his life.

Another competitor was asked how he was.

"I'm in great shape," he replied. "From the ankle up."

• The Bunion Derby had all sorts of financial setbacks. Spectators were charged admission to watch the start at Ascot Speedway Stadium, but the promoter, Charles Pyle, soon found that people refused to pay when they could see the race for free on the open road. The race didn't bring in as much money as Pyle had hoped.

• Pyle collected money from towns where the runners stayed overnight, but the cost of accommodation and food drained finances further, and the cooks walked out at one point in the race. At the end, there was some doubt whether Pyle even had enough to pay the prize money.

• When Andy Payne received his prize money, he used it to pay off the mortgage on his father's farm in Claremore, Oklahoma. He retired from running immediately.

• Unbelievably, Charles Pyle organized a second Bunion Derby for the following year. This time 91 runners started from New York and ran 3,685 miles to Los Angeles in 78 days. The race had an incredible ending. Peter Gavuzzi of England started the last lap in the lead, but John Salo, second in 1928, overtook him and won by a mere three minutes. Nineteen runners finished the race.

• John Salo's prize money – $10,000 the first year and $25,000 the second year – made him a wealthy man. However, Salo died in 1930 in a freak accident.

• Charles Pyle was also known for organizing a marathon walking race from coast to coast. After a while, he stopped organizing long-distance foot races and turned to dance marathons.

Marathons

1. Arvind Pandya (India) ran across the United States, from Los Angeles to New York City, in 107 days in 1984. Pandya's time was slower than that of the Bunion Derby winners of the late 1920s, but this was hardly surprising – he was running backwards!

2. The annual Marathon des Sables takes place over 220 km of the Sahara Desert in scorching temperatures of around 35°C (96°F). The daily stages vary from 15 km to 75 km. Competitors risk hazards including heat exhaustion, dehydration, and exposure to sandstorms.

3. Dance marathons became a craze in the late 1920s and early 1930s as people became desperate to raise money. Horace McCoy's story, *They Shoot Horses, Don't They?* describes how contestants had to continue moving night and day in a gruelling test of endurance, stopping only for ten-minute breaks every hour and 50 minutes. They learned to sleep on each other's shoulders as they danced.

4. The oldest bicycle marathon is the Tour de France, which started in 1903. The longest-ever tour was in 1919, when riders cycled 5,380 km in 15 days.

5. There is now a regular bicycle race across the United States. One year Paul Selon covered the 5,000 km from California to New York in 200 hours and 45 minutes.

6. In 1927, in the era of marathons, Doe Grahame set off from Mobile Golf Club, Alabama, to play golf to the west coast of the United States, a distance of over 3,000 miles. He completed the first 850 miles, to San Antonio, Texas, in 10,930 strokes, having lost 105 balls!

7. Greek runner Yiannis Louros holds both world records for 1,000 km and 1,000 miles. Sandra Barwick holds the women's record for these distances.

8. In 1930, Fred Newton swam 2,938 km down the Mississippi River in the United States, staying in the water for an amazing 742 hours. It took him six months!

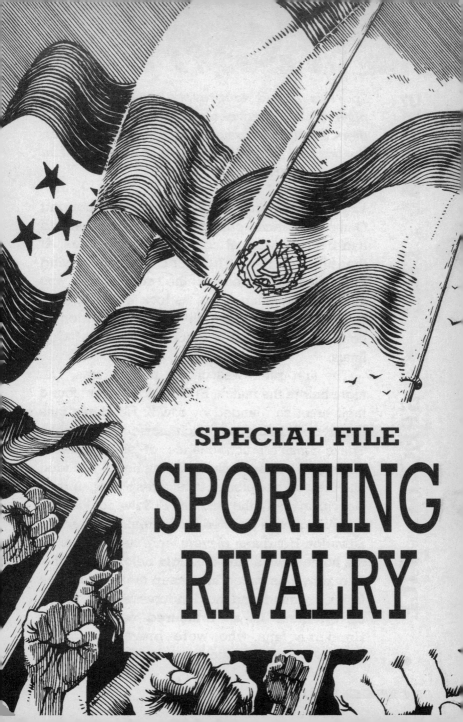

SPECIAL FILE

SPORTING RIVALRY

Sport is bound to provoke rivalry between players, and between the fans who support them. But it isn't always good-natured. And when politics and sport come together, the result can be all-out war...

1. Honduras and El Salvador, neighbouring Central American countries, were old rivals and had been in political conflict for many years. At the time of the 1970 World Cup qualifying matches, tension between the two countries was almost at breaking point. As luck would have it, Honduras were drawn to play El Salvador, at home and away, for a place in the World Cup finals.

The first game was played in Honduras. The night before the match, El Salvador players found their hotel surrounded by rowdy Honduras fans intent on making as much noise as possible. There wasn't much chance of sleep for the players as whistles shrilled, car horns sounded and fireworks exploded in an ear-splitting uproar. Not surprisingly, the next day El Salvador lost 1-0.

Revenge was planned for the return game in El Salvador. Honduras players were kept awake by the home team's fans the night before the game. The army was called in to keep the peace at the football ground, and the Honduras team had to be driven there in an armoured car! The few Honduran fans who were brave enough to actually go to the match were attacked, and two were killed. Such was the hostility of the El Salvador crowd, Honduras felt quite relieved at their 3-0 defeat.

Meanwhile, the political situation deteriorated and the two governments were about to go to war. This did nothing for the mood of the crowd at the play-off game, which took place in Mexico for safety reasons. Five thousand police were brought in, and trouble was kept to a minimum. After extra time, El Salvador won the match 3-2. The authorities managed to separate the jubilant, jeering El Salvador fans from the dejected Hondurans, and the fans went home to their respective countries.

The football match mirrored a conflict which wasn't resolved so easily: a few days later, Honduras and El Salvador were at war.

2. When the England rugby league team toured Australia in 1954, their match against New South Wales had to be abandoned because of violence on the pitch. A number of players became involved in an out-and-out brawl that rapidly became completely out of control. The shame-faced players all agreed they had been very silly indeed, and when they met in a test match the following week they kissed and made up afterwards.

3. In 1940, citizens of Venezuela and Santo Domingo demanded that their governments

declare war on one another over a baseball match! The result of the match had been settled by an umpire's decision, which fans thought was unfair. Fortunately, things didn't go that far, but the two countries remained hostile to one another for a long time afterwards.

4. The Irish FA Cup semi-final between Glentoran and Belfast Celtic in 1920 came at a time of severe political unrest in Ireland. A player was sent off shortly before the final whistle was due, which proved too much for the over-excited fans. The referee found himself the target of a hail of stones. The crowd went berserk and one man wielded a gun and began shooting. Several people were injured, and the match was abandoned without a replay.

5. In 1956 the Soviet Union sent troops to Hungary to quell a revolt. The two countries met a month later in a water-polo match in the Olympic Games, which soon degenerated into a fight between the players. The referee was forced to abandon the match, and police had to be called in to prevent a riot in the crowd.

SKIING

The Eagle Has Landed

Eddie "the Eagle" Edwards soared to fame at the 1988 Winter Olympics – but not because he was a brilliant skier. Eddie won so much media attention, and the hearts of thousands of fans, because he captured the true spirit of competition...

Calgary, Alberta, Canada, 14 February and 23 February 1988

It was late in the evening when an unlikely hero stepped off the plane and walked into the airport in Calgary, Canada. With his thick glasses and short, stocky frame he didn't look much like a sports star.

Eddie Edwards had arrived in Calgary from Britain for the ski-jump competitions at the Winter Olympics. He didn't expect to win, he was just pleased to be there. He wasn't good enough to attract much publicity, but, as it happened, media attention turned to him for other reasons. Soon, the whole world would know about him. It became the biggest event of his life.

Accident-prone Eddie walked through customs desperately trying to stuff his clothes back into his burst suitcase. He was amazed to discover a crowd of people waiting for him. His fans rang cow-bells and waved a seven-metre banner:

"Welcome to Eddie the Eagle Edwards."

Wow, that's brilliant, he thought to himself. He didn't know he had a fan club in Canada. He couldn't take his eyes off the banner. In fact, he was still looking at it when he walked into a plate-glass door.

It was now very late in the evening and he needed to find an

official connected to the British Olympic ski team. That took more time. Then, together with the official, Eddie set off for the Olympic village. It was 2 am when they finally arrived.

The next morning Eddie Edwards missed most of the practice because he was sorting out equipment problems and making more arrangements. He was even an hour late for his press conference.

"You can't come in here," said a security man on the door. "There's a press conference for Eddie Edwards."

"But I am Eddie Edwards."

"You? No, never. You're not an athlete."

The security man finally let him in and Eddie Edwards faced questions from 130 journalists.

"Do you wear your glasses for jumping, Eddie?"

"Yes. They mist up when I put my goggles on. I just hope they clear by the time I reach the bottom."

The journalists soon took to the skier's friendly grin and the stories of his various scrapes. Eddie Edwards told them all about how he became a ski-jumper despite the fact that Britain had no history of producing ski-jumpers. He told the journalists about his struggles to get started, and how he had slept in scout centres and mental hospitals, or in his van in freezing weather, while competing in other countries. Anything to save money. He also told them about his injuries. Eddie Edwards had been fighting back from injury ever since he was 11 when he twisted his knee in the playground and had to spend three months in hospital.

"Hey, is it true you once tied up your jaw?" one journalist asked him.

"I hit the ground with a crash and took most of the impact

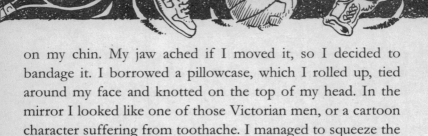

on my chin. My jaw ached if I moved it, so I decided to bandage it. I borrowed a pillowcase, which I rolled up, tied around my face and knotted on the top of my head. In the mirror I looked like one of those Victorian men, or a cartoon character suffering from toothache. I managed to squeeze the helmet on, and off I set."

Eddie had stories of working on building sites to make money to enter the next skiing competition. He had scrimped and saved to go on his first school skiing trip and then, on his first day on the slopes, he had fallen over four or five times. Having got the skiing bug, he spent school lessons drawing skiers and writing about skiing, and he spent most of his spare time on an artificial ski slope in Gloucester.

The journalists didn't know what to make of him. They could see that he was short-sighted, broke and accident-prone. What was he doing at the Winter Olympics? He had no chance of winning. Was he a figure of fun who didn't deserve to be there? Or was he an amateur in the true Olympic tradition, someone who was there to compete rather than to win? He made a refreshing change from the serious approach of most other athletes, anyway. He showed that sport can be fun. You have to train hard and be sensible, but you can enjoy it whether you win or lose.

The journalists fired questions at him for an hour.

"Is this guy for real?" one finally said.

Eddie was enjoying the attention. He was enjoying being there.

The journalists and the rest of the world couldn't wait to see him in action. Some of the other competitors weren't so sure. Some had trained for 20 years to get to the Olympics and now

a young upstart with no chance of winning had come along to steal the limelight. Some of the other competitors wanted Eddie to take a running jump rather than a ski-jump.

Then came the day of the first competition.

There are two ski-jump events at the Winter Olympics. The 70 metres was the first to take place, while the 90 metres would follow a few days later.

As Eddie Edwards made his way to the top of the mountain for the 70 metre jump, he heard the names and distances of the other competitors announced.

"Lotric of Yugoslavia … 85 metres."

"Collins of Canada … 83.5 metres."

Eddie Edwards knew he had no chance of jumping anywhere near that distance. He hadn't jumped anything like that from a height of 90 metres, let alone 70 metres.

Eddie was twenty-fourth to jump that day and was certain of setting a record – he was Britain's first-ever Olympic competitor in the 70 metre ski-jump. At the top of the mountain he took in the scene. Below were 40,000 spectators. Scattered around were many television cameras. Anything could happen. There was a good chance he would make a fool of himself. But he'd got there, he'd got to the Olympics and he was taking part. How many others could say that?

Eddie Edwards squatted down, pushed off and began to slide over the snow, faster and faster. As his goggles misted over he concentrated on keeping his skis straight. He could feel the icy cold wind on his face. He was ready to lift off.

Some said that Eddie the Eagle didn't jump, he dropped out of the sky. He was still a long time coming down, alone in the air, flapping his arms, working for distance.

"Edwards of Great Britain ... 55 metres."

It was good enough for last place.

Matti Nykanen of Finland had jumped 89.5 metres, so Eddie's performance was laughable to some people.

By his second jump he was enjoying the competition even more. He waved to the crowd, winked at the camera and launched himself towards more fame.

"Edwards of Great Britain ... 55 metres."

No improvement.

A week later, in the 90 metre ski-jump competition, on a clear, crisp day with no wind, Eddie Edwards jumped a new British record of 71 metres in front of 80,000 spectators. He was delighted, even if Nykanen had managed 118.5 metres to win the gold medal.

The day after the 90 metre competition, Eddie Edwards was more popular than the gold medallist. He was invited on chat shows, and people wanted him to open events. He was invited to sing on records in England and Finland. Why was he in demand? It was probably because he was just an ordinary person, a gallant loser who celebrated failure rather than success. He was a true amateur who finished a glorious last. Yet he showed he could do something that most people would never do – he could get to the Olympics.

• Ski-jump competitors are awarded points for distance jumped, and style. Eddie Edwards scored very badly on style in 1988. In fact, in the 70 metre jump competition, his total point score was less than half that of any other competitor.

• For the first time at a Winter Olympics, the Calgary Games included a team ski-jump event, but Eddie Edwards couldn't compete because he was the only British ski-jumper there! Matti Nykanen won his third gold medal of the Games as a member of the winning Finnish team.

• Sadly, after 1988, the Olympic ski-jump standards were raised beyond the qualification standards of gallant losers like Eddie Edwards.

Winter Olympics

1. The 1924 Olympic ski-jump competition had an error in the addition of one competitor's score. The error wasn't discovered until 50 years later. Thorleif Houg, long deceased, was demoted from third place to fourth, and Anders Haugen was promoted from fourth to third. Haugen was presented with a bronze medal at a special ceremony. By then he was 83 years old!

2. On several occasions, the longest ski-jump has gone unrewarded because of points dropped for style. At the 1928 Winter Olympics, the competitor with the longest jump finished twenty-eighth because he fell on landing.

3. At the 1948 Winter Olympics, Swedish speed skater Åke Seyffarth won gold at 10,000 metres and silver at 1,500 metres. He was expected to win the 5,000 metre race too, but bumped into a photographer who was on the ice trying to get a good action shot! Seyffarth had been in the lead, but came in seventh because of the time he'd lost.

4. Another speed skater, American Dan Jansen, was tipped to win gold in two skating events at the 1988 Olympics. He fell over in both, and had to wait until the 1994 Olympics for another chance. Amazingly, he slipped *again* in one of the 1994

events and lost another possible medal. But he did get a gold in the 1,000 metres speed skating that year – at last!

5. Robin Cousins was a very popular gold medallist in the men's figure skating at the 1980 Winter Olympics. He had skated beautifully, but he didn't look so elegant when he stumbled and fell up the victory platform before receiving his medal!

6. When Katarina Witt won the woman's figure skating gold medal at the 1984 Winter Olympics she received 35,000 love letters.

7. Perhaps the most famous ice figure-skater of all time was Sonja Henie of Norway. At 11, she made her international debut at the first Winter Olympics (1924). She won gold medals at the next three Winter Olympics and was world champion for ten successive years from 1927 to 1936.

8. A very surprising competitor in the 1992 Winter Olympics was a bobsleigh team from Jamaica, a country not famous for its icy conditions! A film, *Cool Runnings,* was even made about the team. Like Eddie the Eagle, the Jamaican bobsleighers have become famous as gallant losers.

EPILOGUE

Sport has changed over the years. The original Olympic ideal – it is not the winning but the taking part that matters – has been overtaken by the quest for victory. Attendance at sports events has been affected by television. Sport has become big business.

Sport certainly requires hard work, but it's about more than that. Talk to retired sports stars and they don't only remember the winning goal or the shot that brings "Game, set and match". They also remember the people they have met, the friendships they have shared and the stories they have heard.

Sport is there to be enjoyed. It is fun to play and a pleasure to watch, whether you're in the Olympic stadium or the school sports hall, and whether you win or lose.